Volume 1

CLARINET SOLOS
with piano accompaniment
arranged and edited by Thea King

INDEX

			Page Score	Part
1.	Il Mio Tesoro	W. A. Mozart	2	2
2.	Trio from Minuet of Octet, Op. 166	F. Schubert	4	2
3.	Allegretto from Quintet for Clarinet, Strings and Piano	J. Labor	6	3
4.	Allegro from Sonata No. 3	X. Lefèvre	9	4
5.	Entr'acte from Carmen	G. Bizet	12	5
6.	Allegretto from Symphony No. 3	F. Schubert	14	5
7.	Allegro Con Grazia from Symphony No. 6	P. Tchaikovsky	15	6
8.	Minuet from Serenade for Wind Octet, K. 375	W. A. Mozart	20	7

WARNING: the photocopying of any pages of this publication is illegal. If copies are made in breach of copyright, the Publishers will, where possible, sue for damages.

Every illegal copy means a lost sale. Lost sales lead to shorter print runs and rising prices. Soon the music goes out of print, and more fine works are lost from the repertoire.

CHESTER MUSIC

(A division of Music Sales Limited)
8/9 Frith Street, London W1V 5TZ
Exclusive distributors: Music Sales Ltd., Newmarket Road
Bury St Edmunds, Suffolk IP33 3YB

PREFACE TO VOLUME ONE
This collection presents original clarinet tunes from various contexts, taken from works by both familiar and lesser-known composers. Some of the instrumental combinations in which they normally appear may not be easily available to the student, so these adaptations with piano could provide suitable pieces for study or performance.

Thea King. 1976.

NOTES

1. Il Mio Tesoro.   Wolfgang Amadeus Mozart, 1756-1791.

   This is the famous tenor aria from *Don Giovanni*, introduced in the opera by clarinet and bassoon, in which Don Ottavio comforts Donna Anna, mourning her father's murder at the hand of Don Giovanni.

2. Trio from The Minuet of Octet, Op. 166.
   Franz Schubert, 1797-1828.

   The original scoring is for clarinet, bassoon, horn, string quartet and double bass, and the clarinet shares this rather swaggering tune with bassoon and first violin.

3. Allegretto from Quintet for Clarinet, Strings and Piano, Op. 11.
   Josef Labor, 1842-1924.

   Labor was a blind Bohemian musician who worked in Hanover and Vienna and was a composer of church and chamber music. This theme comes from Quintet for clarinet, string trio and piano, and one of his more famous pupils, Franz Schmidt (1874-1939), used it for a set of variations in a quintet for the very same combination.

4. Allegro from Sonata No. 3.   Xavier Lefèvre, 1763-1829.

   Lefèvre lived most of his life in Paris and did much to develop the keywork of the clarinet besides composing teaching material and works for wind instruments. He wrote two sets of sonatas, published for clarinet and bass instruments. I have realised this movement with piano, but the bass line could be played by bassoon or cello to make an attractive duo.

5. Entr'acte from Carmen.   Georges Bizet, 1838-1875.

   This interlude is played before Act 3, and is a duet for flute and clarinet, with occasional comments from the cor anglais. The accompaniment is very imaginative and delicate, with the harp adding its special colour throughout.

6. Allegretto from Symphony No. 3.   Franz Schubert, 1797-1828.

   This winsome tune appears in the middle of the slow movement of the symphony, written when Schubert was only eighteen. The orchestral part is usually printed for clarinet in C (which the player then transposes up a tone on the B♭ clarinet); the accompaniment is played pizzicato by the strings.

7. Allegro Con Grazia from Symphony No. 6.
   Peter Tchaikovsky, 1840-1893.

   This famous movement, here shortened, from the *Pathetic Symphony* is probably the most successful ever written in 5/4 time and it is quite fascinating to play and to listen to. In the orchestra the A clarinet is used, so the piano part has been adjusted to suit the B♭ clarinet.

8. Minuet from Serenade for Wind Octet, K. 375.
   Wolfgang Amadeus Mozart, 1756-1791.

   There are two versions of this serenade; the first was for a sextet of clarinets, bassoons and horns, and later Mozart added oboes. In both versions this movement features the clarinet, whose part is exactly as printed here.

1
Il Mio Tesoro

MOZART

© Copyright 1977, 1989 Chester Music Ltd.,
8/9 Frith Street, London. W1V 5TZ

All rights reserved

2
Trio from the Minuet of Octet, Op. 166

SCHUBERT

3

Allegretto from Quintet for Clarinet, Strings and Piano

LABOR

4
From Sonata No. 3

LEFÈVRE

Volume 1

CLARINET SOLOS
with piano accompaniment
arranged and edited by Thea King

INDEX

			Page Score	Part
1.	Il Mio Tesoro	W. A. Mozart	2	2
2.	Trio from Minuet of Octet, Op. 166	F. Schubert	4	2
3.	Allegretto from Quintet for Clarinet, Strings and Piano	J. Labor	6	3
4.	Allegro from Sonata No. 3	X. Lefèvre	9	4
5.	Entr'acte from Carmen	G. Bizet	12	5
6.	Allegretto from Symphony No. 3	F. Schubert	14	5
7.	Allegro Con Grazia from Symphony No. 6	P. Tchaikovsky	15	6
8.	Minuet from Serenade for Wind Octet, K. 375	W. A. Mozart	20	7

WARNING: the photocopying of any pages of this publication is illegal. If copies are made in breach of copyright, the Publishers will, where possible, sue for damages.

Every illegal copy means a lost sale. Lost sales lead to shorter print runs and rising prices. Soon the music goes out of print, and more fine works are lost from the repertoire.

CHESTER MUSIC

(A division of Music Sales Limited)
8/9 Frith Street, London W1V 5TZ

1
Il Mio Tesoro

MOZART

2
Trio from the Minuet of Octet, Op. 166

SCHUBERT

© Copyright 1977, 1989 Chester Music Ltd.,
8/9 Frith Street, London. W1V 5TZ

All rights reserved

3
Allegretto from Quintet for Clarinet, Strings and Piano

Allegretto grazioso

LABOR

4
From Sonata No. 3
LEFÈVRE

5
Entr'acte from Carmen

BIZET

6
Allegretto from Symphony No. 3

SCHUBERT

7
Allegro Con Grazia from Symphony No. 6

TCHAIKOVSKY

8
Minuet from Serenade for Wind Octet, K. 375
MOZART

SELECTED MUSIC FOR CLARINET AND PIANO

BÄCK	Elegy
BAKER	Cantilena
BOYLE	Sonatina
DEBUSSY	Première Rhapsodie
DEBUSSY	Two Pieces
FALLA	Two Pieces from *El Amor Brujo*
GADE	Fantasy Pieces Op. 43
HOROWITZ	Concertino for Clarinet and Strings
KALLIWODA	Morceau de Salon Op. 299
LAZARUS/LOVREGLIO	Two Operatic Fantasias
LUTOSLAWSKI	Dance Preludes
MACONCHY	Fantasia for Clarinet and Piano
MOZART	Divertimento No 1 (from K439b)
MOZART	Divertimento No 2 (from K439b)
MOZART	Divertimento No 3 (from K439b)
OBERTHUR	Le Désir
POULENC	Sonata
SAINT-SAËNS	Sonata
SZALOWSKI	Sonatina
STANFORD	Three Intermezzi
WATERSON	Morceau de Concert
WOOD	Paraphrase

SOLO CLARINET

BENTZON	Theme and Variations Op. 14
BERKELEY	Three Pieces
MORTENSEN	Sonatina Op. 9
STRAVINSKY	Three Pieces

From

CHESTER MUSIC

(A division of Music Sales Limited)
8/9 Frith Street, London W1V 5TZ

5
Entr'acte from Carmen

BIZET

6
Allegretto from Symphony No. 3

SCHUBERT

7
Allegro Con Grazia from Symphony No. 6

Allegro con grazia ♩=144

TCHAIKOVSKY

8
Minuet from Serenade for Wind Octet, K. 375

Allegro

MOZART

Flute	Editor: Trevor Wye		Clarinet	Editor: Thea King
Oboe	Editor: James Brown		Bassoon	Editor: William Waterhouse
	Saxophone	Editor: Paul Harvey		

A growing collection of volumes from Chester Music, containing a
wide range of pieces from different periods.

CLARINET SOLOS VOLUME I

Bizet	Entr'acte from Carmen
Labor	Allegretto from Quintet for Clarinet, Strings and Piano
Lefèvre	Allegro from Sonata No. 3
Mozart	Minuet from Serenade for Wind Octet K. 375
Mozart	Il Mio Tesoro
Schubert	Trio from the Minuet of Octet, Op. 166
Schubert	Allegretto from Symphony No. 3
Tchaikovsky	Allegro Con Grazia from Symphony No. 6

CLARINET SOLOS VOLUME II

Beethoven	Allegro (Finale) from Wind Sextet Op. 71
Crusell	Minuet from Quartet in C minor Op. 4
Crusell	Andante Moderato from Concerto in B♭ Op. 1
Glazounov	Allegretto from the ballet The Seasons
Mendelssohn	Andante from Konzertstück in D minor Op. 114
Molter	Moderato from Concerto in D
Rimsky-Korsakov	Andante from Concerto for Clarinet and Military Band
Weber	From Introduction, Theme and Variations

Also available:
CLARINET DUETS VOLUMES I, II & III
Further details on request

CHESTER MUSIC

(A division of Music Sales Limited)
8/9 Frith Street, London W1V 5TZ